PAST
PRAYER
MINISTRY
TRAINING

Mary Pytches & Prue Bedwell

Published By New Wine Publishing
4A Ridley Avenue, Ealing, London W13 9XW
ISBN 978 1 9029 7703 4
© Mary Pytches/Prue Bedwell/New Wine
First Published October 1997
New Wine edition July 1999
2nd Edition May 2005
Reprint July 2012
Acknowledgements
All scripture quotations are taken from the Holy Bible New International Version,
copyright © 1973, 1978, 1984 by International Bible Society. used with permission of
Hodder and Stoughton a member of the Hodder Headline Group. All rights reserved.
NIV is a trade mark of International Bible Society, UK trade mark number 1448790
A catalogue record for this book is available from the British Library
Type set Mike Thorpe, Design Chapel
Cover design New Wine
Printed in Great Britain by Halcyon

Contents

Introduction

Every church has pastoral responsibility for its own membership. This includes supporting the physically sick, bereaved or troubled people in its care. Many churches these days provide a prayer ministry team who operate after the Sunday services and pray for people's needs, physical, emotional and spiritual. On occasions the problem is more complicated and the person would benefit from longer term help. In many churches, the overworked and hard-pressed leader will then try and see them. However, in most congregations there are usually some mature Christians who could happily take on this ministry. They are submissive to authority, good listeners, have a wide knowledge of the Bible, are people of prayer and have an understanding of the work of the Holy Spirit. They are also in a good position to give some godly counsel, all of which could be very beneficial. Though ti may be helpful to have had some counselling training, this is not absolutely necessary and in any case it may not be affordable or feasible time-wise. Therefore it is better not to call such a ministry counselling. It is a pastoral prayer ministry.

This booklet is an introduction to such a ministry. It is the outline for a teaching day which presents the nuts and bolts for setting up a pastoral prayer ministry in a local church. Not every church is the same and the guidelines set out in this booklet are just that. Each church has to work things out to suit its own congregation. Our prayer is that the teaching will be helpful and serve as a jumping off place for those wanting to be involved in the pastoral care of the Church.

Mary Pytches and **Prue Bedwell**

Guidelines for Pastoral Prayer Ministry

Pastoral Prayer Ministry in the Church is co-ordinated by the leadership's appointed co-ordinator.

When any request comes to the co-ordinator, an initial interview is arranged to decide whether prayer should be offered and who should see the person wanting ministry.

Newcomers to the church are encouraged initially to get involved in the life of the church, join a home group and be open to the work of the Holy Spirit, Sunday by Sunday.

Planned prayer sessions are not offered to those being medically treated without reference to the doctor concerned. Prayer support, but not in-depth ministry, may be given to someone undergoing psychotherapy.

Pastoral prayer is undertaken in twos, either two women or a husband and wife team, or, in the case of a man, it may be two men. Team members are discouraged from praying in partnership with a married member of the opposite sex other than one's spouse for any extended ministry. Praying with members of the opposite sex alone is not approved.

The co-ordinator will see that each praying couple is supervised on a regular basis by appointed supervisors. The supervisor is understood to be part of the confidential group, but not involved in ministry.

Three to four sessions are offered followed by a review, which allows for a termination, a break, a referral or the continuation of the defined period of prayer sessions.

Unless otherwise requested by the leadership, pastoral prayer ministry is only offered to a member of the church, ie one who has attended for some months and belongs to a home group.

If a praying couple takes on an individual from outside the membership, unless requested by the church leadership, this is seen as outside the authority and supervisory structure of the church. The couple take personal responsibility for such prayer, but it is felt to be unwise to do this without consulting the co-ordinator.

Use of a prayer room on church premises is encouraged, if possible. This will need to be booked up ahead of time, but any 'safe place' is suitable.

One and a half hours is the normal time spent with an individual.

Ministry after 10pm is discouraged. Brief records are maintained by prayer couples. They are not copied or held centrally and they are kept confidential. Every six months there is a review of who is being seen. In this way the overloading of any prayer couple is avoided.

Qualities of those ministering

Requirements for those ministering
- An intuitive understanding of human nature
- Good common sense
- Experience of life
- A high degree of interest in people generally
- An ability to focus fully on another and enter into his/her world
- A natural aptitude
- A Holy Spirit anointing for the work
- A regular member of the prayer ministry team

Attitude towards the one coming for prayer
- To be real
- To be warm and accepting
- To show empathy

Spiritual qualities
- A personal knowledge and relationship with Jesus (1 John 2:3)
- An increasing knowledge of the Word of God (Col. 3:16)
- An understanding of the authority that pertains to a disciple of Christ (John 20:22-23)
- An empowering of the Holy spirit and an openness to His continual anointing (Acts 18)
- A facility for hearing God (John 5:19)
- A personal desire for wholeness oneself (Matt. 7:4-5)

Counter-productive characteristics
- A need to be needed
- Emotional instability
- A judgmental attitude
- Inability to keep a confidence

People's problems and their causes

Introduction

The objective of pastoral prayer ministry:
To be changed into the image of Jesus and to grow in maturity.
Rom. 8:29
Eph. 4:13-16
BUT blockages to growth may occur. Such as:
- Anxiety and panic attacks
- Depression
- Fear of rejection
- Angry outbursts
- Sexual neurosis
- Low self-esteem
- Insecurity
- Relationship problems

How can we bring healing and change into people's lives?

Understanding the cause of the problem is a help.
Understanding doesn't heal, but it does give us a key to healing.

An iceberg, showing the ABC of feelings gives simple understanding (taken and adapted from Albert Ellis's Rational Emotive Therapy). Only a small percentage of an iceberg is above the water line. The rest is hidden beneath the waves. Similarly a lot of what goes on in a person's life lies in the unconscious.

Consequences ('C') or patterns of behaviour are fairly obvious.

Beliefs and Feelings ('B') are not always obvious. These are what motivate our behaviour.

An Activating Event or Events ('A'). These are events which stimulate our emotions and form our thinking.

'A' – Activating Events

First remember:

i. We live in fallen world
ii. We are fallen people
    Our parents were imperfect, as were their parents (getting stuck in blame will get us nowhere)
iii. We have inherited some family characteristics
iv. We have an enemy who is against our wholeness

Bearing these in mind the Activating Events (traumas) which may cause problems later are those that happen within a dysfunctional family system.

1. A Dysfunctional Family is one in which:

i. Basic needs are not met
   Basic needs = Security, Self worth and Significance (3 S's – Selwyn Hughes)
   This leaves people with an emotional vacuum
ii. Poor modelling and teaching are absorbed
iii. Traumatic experiences remain unresolved due to poor communication.
    'The family that feels together, heals together.'

2. Possible Traumatic Events

Some of the worst traumas involve loss – of some sort.

i. Loss of value and security through loss of welcome
   Every child needs to feel welcomed; first in the womb and then on arrival.
ii. Loss of security through separation or abandonment
    Too early or too sudden a separation from source of nurture (mother) can be like an emotional death to a small child.
iii. Loss of care through death of a parent

iv.   Loss of childhood.
      Abuse, constant anxiety, and inappropriate responsibility can rob a child of
      his/her childhood

v.   Loss of value through rejection.
      Whether at home, or outside the home, rejection is always devastating.
      'Our greatest need is acceptance and our greatest fear is rejection.' (Anon)

vi.   Loss of value through shaming.
      This may be through accident, circumstances, ignorance, another person's sin.

vii. Loss of affirmation
      Fathers are important to their children throughout childhood, but especially at
      puberty when they are able, better than mothers, to affirm their children's
      personhood and sexuality.

Conclusion

Bad things happen to all of us as we are growing up. In a home where communication
is good there is healing along the way, but when a child has not been allowed to express
his feelings and talk about his traumatic experience the pain remains buried. These
unresolved issues bring consequences.

Possible ways through:
• Isaiah 61:1,2 '...to bind up the broken hearted... to comfort all who mourn'.
• Open up the hurt and pain to Jesus.
• Ask Him for healing.
• Forgive those who may have caused the trauma.

The consequences of unresolved trauma

Introduction

We are called to become like Jesus

Romans 8:29 '...to be conformed to the likeness of his Son'.

Paul tells us to continue to work at our wholeness.

'Therefore my friends ... continue to work out your salvation, (or 'wholeness', from the Greek word 'sozo'), with fear and trembling, for it is God who works in you to will and to act according to his good purpose.' (Phil 2:12,13)

Ministry is aimed at removing the blockages that prevent this happening.

'Therefore strengthen your feeble arms and weak knees. Make level paths for your feet so that the lame may not be disabled but rather be healed.' (Heb 12:12)

Look again at the diagram of the iceberg.

Having looked at 'A', Activating Events, now move up the iceberg to the 'B', (Beliefs and Feelings) and to 'C', (the Consequences).

Strategies for Survival

As a result of unresolved trauma children (and adults) form unconscious strategies, or coping mechanisms, for survival. The goal is to avoid or ease discomfort. These strategies may be useful in childhood, but as life goes on the behaviour tends to inhibit growth, and can cause difficulties. change may be quite hard to effect, because to an extent, the strategies work, in so far as they protect from perceived danger, and what is more they feel normal.

Examples of possible strategies (taken from *Dying to Change* by Mary Pytches)

Remember: we are all different and though the trauma may be similar, we will find different ways of coping with it according to our personalities.

The Armadillo

Abandonment, abuse, separation or rejection may cause a person to build a protective shell around their feelings. The objective is not to be hurt ever again. Intimate relationships, receiving love, and making commitments, are all perceived as dangerous and produce fear. 'People are not there when needed', and 'people are not to be trusted' are the unconscious thoughts.

The Prickly Pear

This person may have experienced similar traumas as 'The Armadillo', but rejection is the dominant feeling, therefore the coping mechanism is aimed at avoiding any further rejection. People are perceived as dangerous and hostility keeps the danger away.

Top Dog

This person has probably experienced being in the terrifying position of being controlled by someone bigger and stronger, as in abuse, or bullying. The strategy is to become the one 'in control'. Spontaneity and flexibility are sacrificed for security. Anger and fear result if this control is threatened. The extreme of this strategy is Obsessive Compulsive Disorder (OCD), where controlling an element of the environment or one's experience of life reduces anxiety.

The St. Bernard Dog

This is the 'compulsive rescuer', usually the result of a chaotic childhood, where anxiety was eased by trying to rescue the situation. This way of coping may have been encouraged by the needy parent, therefore the behaviour was endorsed and gradually became the habitual response to any situation that has within it echoes of the past. 'I must resolve, rescue, be responsible,' is the recurring theme.

The Clinging Ivy

This is the 'relationship addict' who eases the fear of being abandoned or rejected yet again by making dependent relationships. The need to gain and hold attention can lead to some rather hysterical behaviour.
(It is easier to become an addict to almost anything if there is a void to be filled.)

The Proud Wriggler

When not enough encouragement or affirmation is given a child may lack an appropriate sense of value. Valid or not, criticism of even the mildest sort, can cause such a person to become very defensive. The goal is to protect the already damaged self. One way of doing this is to point an accusing finger back at the person giving the criticism.

The Rat Racer

Another way of dealing with a damaged self-esteem is to become a 'somebody'. It is achievement at all costs. 'I will be valued if I perform well', is the motivation. Such a person may even sacrifice family and friends on the altar of success.

The Perfectionist

Lack of encouragement and praise in childhood can cause a person to spend a lifetime trying to win the longed-for approval. Constant anxiety and fear motivates them into performing perfectly. 'I must get it right' dominates their thinking.

The Grace Killer

Criticisms and unhelpful comparisons can make a child long, for once, to be the best. 'If I am good, if I am better than ... I will be loved and valued.' So begins the habit of rule keeping (usually self-made ones) that makes this person feel better, or at least better than those who don't keep them.

The People Pleaser

A childhood of trying desperately to live up to expectations can cause someone, in adulthood, to live with a constant need to please. The equation that dominates their thinking is, 'my self worth depends on what other people think of me.'

The Clown

Rejection, 'put-downs', and teasing can cause a child to think that they are unacceptable. They then develop the strategy of hiding their real selves behind a mask which will be pleasing to everyone. They become the 'life and soul of the party', but 'if people really knew me they wouldn't like me' is the message that controls their behaviour.

The Problem with these strategies

Survival strategies tend to be static and change is an essential part of being a Christian. To pursue comfort and ease are not Christian goals (Matthew 6:33).

They are ways of getting our basic needs met apart from God who wants to meet those needs in His way. 'My people have committed two sins: They have forsaken me, the spring of living water, and have dug their own cisterns, broken cisterns that cannot hold water.' (Jer 2:13).

They take the edge off our hunger for God. It is the hungry that are filled with good things (Luke 1:53).

Possible ways through:
• Acknowledge the survival mechanism
• Repent
• Call out to God for help to change
• Work on changing beliefs and behaviour

Some irrational beliefs

I am responsible for other people's happiness

I must play a role in order to be accepted

This is the way I am and always will be

Love does not last

I must keep the peace at all costs

If people really knew me they would not like me

If I avoid looking at problems they will go away

Men are untrustworthy

Women are illogical and emotional

Conflict is always bad

It is wrong to waste time on myself

I must never make a mistake

I am a failure

It is wrong to need other people

Whatever I do I should do perfectly

If I want something done I have to do it myself

My happiness depends on others

My happiness depends on being loved

It is important to be accepted by others

I must work hard to be accepted by others

Practices in Pastoral Prayer Ministry

Basic Guidelines

Quiet room – 'do not disturb' sign
Water – Kleenex
Length of session, one-two hours
Four sessions to start then review
Harmony between the prayer couple

Exploration Time

Listen to God, listen to the person
Ask:
Presenting problem
Past history – to present day
Physical condition
Spiritual condition

Listen and Watch for:

Belief system (which may be material)
Feelings expressed
Behaviour patterns (choices)
Repetitive dreams
Body language
Reflect back

Prayer Time

Pray and welcome the Holy Spirit
Encourage counsellee to do the same
Wait
Ask: – What is happening? Any pictures, memories, feelings?
Remember that the feelings connect present with past
Expect God to gift you with gifts of the Spirit
Offer these gifts humbly – you could be wrong!

Resolutions

Possibilities:

Repentance – confess and ask God to forgive

Forgiveness – to those who have hurt us

Renounce inner vows, irrational beliefs

Break curses, hurtful judgements

Deliverance from demonic oppression

Break soul tie or bondage to a relative in Jesus' name

Ask Jesus to come and heal

Give plenty of time

Post Prayer Guidance

Let the individual talk about the ministry

Give help where needed with goals or things to be achieved (behaviour change)

Explain not to go to others for ministry

Be supported by home group

Permission to phone if in pain or anxiety

Give homework, e.g. Ps. 139 or Eph. 1:3-11

Read helpful books

Do something creative: paint, sing, sew, cook, garden etc.

Two-way prayer journal: writing to God and waiting for his reply.

Make sure they know date and time of next appointment

Important –

When you next see them, make sure they know you accept them anyway.

Guidelines for forgiveness

Definition

Forgiveness means that we:

Stop feeling resentment against someone who has hurt us.

Cancel a person's record with us and transfer the responsibility for any punishment to God.

Reasons why we forgive

Because in Christ God forgave us and restored our relationship with Him. (Eph. 4:32).

Because Christ taught that we must forgive. (Matt. 18).

Because forgiveness helps us to be Christ-like.

Because forgiveness restores the present, heals for the future, releases from the past.

Because forgiveness enables us to empty our hearts of hatred.

Because forgiveness opens us to Christ's power to be healed.

Forgiveness when we have sinned

Acknowledge and confess sin to God – maybe in the presence of someone else.

Turn away from the behaviour, attitudes and choices which have been sinful.

Receive forgiveness and cleansing which flows from the cross.

Also, we need to forgive ourselves.

Forgiveness when we have been sinned against

Ask God (by His Holy spirit) to show us the root cause of the hurt.

Express to God the pain of the hurt.

Resolve to forgive the person for the action and the attitude that cause the hurt.

Ask God to forgive the person for the hurt they caused.

Ask God to forgive you for the sins of bitterness, anger, etc.

Bless the person and whenever you think of them again bless them, even in their absence.

Ask the Holy Spirit to come and heal the hurt.

Even if the person is dead, forgive them.

Results of Forgiveness

Emotional, physical, mental and social healing.

Guidelines for deliverance

Introduction

Deliverance ministry can occur at any time during healing ministry or pastoral prayer ministry. This ministry may range from 'speaking to any darkness' in a particular situation without reference to a demonic spirit, to a carefully prepared ministry session with the leadership involved for something as serious as exorcism.

Guidelines

The ministry of deliverance or the healing of the oppressed is part of Christ's commission to his disciples.

The authority for this ministry is delegated by the leadership to authorised members of the healing ministry teams and pastoral prayer ministry teams. It is a trust which is to be exercised responsibly and under authority.

Demons do exist. People can only be delivered by the power of God. No drug, hospital treatment or prison sentence can 'deliver' such cases. The Church alone has the power delegated by God.

Ministry in this area is guided by our values – especially regarding the dignity of the individual, and love for the demonised person.

No deliverance ministry should take place without the recognition and agreement of the individual involved who needs to take a responsible part in this. They need to understand the implication of the ministry and be willing and prepared for it.

No ministry of this nature should be offered to anyone who is already receiving prayer or counselling from someone else or who is under professional support and medication without the prior advice and agreement of the other parties involved.

Any major deliverance intended must be reported to the church leadership before any action is taken. A delay of ministry is seldom a problem – peace can be prayed on the individual and spirits bound to await an appropriate time for this ministry. If someone is believed to be 'possessed', immediate reporting is required.

In all cases we should recognise our limitations. If we are in any doubt, we should delay ministry and seek help and guidance from others.

Individuals should never minister alone. The group involved, where a planned ministry is considered, should include both sexes (with a minimum of three).

Many of the 'apparent symptoms' of oppression could be signs of the Holy Spirit touching deep hurts and not necessarily evidence of demonic activity at all.

Discernment and revelation should be offered sensitively, recognising that the diagnosis and interpretation could be wrong. These need confirmation by others in the ministry team and acceptance by the individual concerned if a deliverance ministry is proposed. Often the individual is also a receiver of discernment and revelation.

Always consider the question of the right time for ministry. Do not continue ministry after about 10 o'clock at night.

Difficulties in Pastoral Prayer Ministry

Dependency

Very common in ministry, especially with a person who has separation anxiety (fears being abandoned or separated from the source of nurture).

Keep good boundaries
Give clear messages
Work with the feelings
Point towards only safe source of comfort – God
May need professional help

Transference

'The displacement of feelings from one object or person to another.'
This will block healing unless worked through.

Recognise it
Look for the person it really belongs to
Do not let counselee get away with it
Use it – it can be useful

Ministering to those with sexual neurosis

Could be:
A homosexual problem: A preference for emotionally intimate relationships with own sex; an ambivalence towards opposite sex; a fear of the opposite sex. Hatred of self.

Pray for will to be strengthened
Work towards counselee coming totally out of denial
Encourage counselee to spend time with God the Father and receive his love
Spend time with counselee worshipping together
Encourage the discipline of relinquishment
Counselee must own up every time he uses his old ways of gaining comfort
Help with re-symbolizing

Take responsibility for the needy part of themselves
Build boundaries around the counselee
Be firm and continually face counselee with truth

Ministry to an abused person

People react to childhood abuse in various ways:

i   In a healthy way because of good support

ii   Others long to be healed. With such:

      Encourage appropriate grieving

      Repeat story until poison is flushed out of system

      Pray for Jesus to come and heal

      Begin the forgiving process

      Some behaviour change may need to be worked on

iii Others become victims. With such:

      Be gentle, but honest

      Help them find their true identity in Christ

      Encourage them to properly grieve but watch for self-pity

      Lead them toward forgiving

      Stop them continually repeating the story

iv   Others live in denial.

      You may suspect abuse – do not suggest it – ever

      First pray that God will show them why they have a problem

      If memory comes back – deal with it (as above)

      If nothing is remembered, leave it

      Continue to pray for healing of whatever caused the presenting problem

      Continue to make it a safe place

Ministering to those wallowing in self-pity

Similar to victim mentality
They must face the truth
They must stop recounting the story and gaining illicit comfort and sympathy as a result
This only delays healing
Once this happens healing can begin

Avoiders of the truth

This could be by:
Rationalising
Tunnel vision
Scapegoating
Compartmentalising

Such people:
Need to feel safe
Need to be built up
Need to feel accepted
Only slowly (or maybe never) will they come to a more truthful position
Repentance is the resolution
Need help with changing behaviour

Case history

First Interview
Questions

Presenting problems

Past history – (through to present)

Physical health –

Spiritual state –

Listen for:

Beliefs (tapes being played) –

Emotions expressed –

Behaviour patterns (choices)

Possible way through (ministry) –

Example of Work sheet (Megan)

Formal Questions to Ask

Presenting problem – Her husband has suggested she looks for help. She has always been a bit of a perfectionist, but recently it has become more pronounced. She is demanding too much of the children and becoming very angry and critical when they do not live up to her standards.

Past History

Middle class family. Older brother who was very close. Dad had great hopes for his children and would get very upset at any failure. He cried when she (Megan) did not pass her college entrance exam. She hated disappointing him. Mum was rather quiet and tried to keep the peace all the time. Dad was rather 'highly strung' and Mum tried to placate him all the time. Megan felt that she was the failure of the family. Even when she married she was afraid she had not pleased her father. he did not actually disapprove of her choice of husband, but never said he approved either. he never praised her for anything. Megan said she felt that she would never please him if she lived to be a hundred!

Her two children, a boy and a girl, were good children. But she hated taking them to her parents' home because her father would always put them them through their paces. If only they had been clever like her brother's children.

Physically

Megan was 35 and appeared to be in good health. She was too thin and rather nervous, had never had a serious illness, had seen the doctor recently about a minor problem and he had pronounced her well.

Spiritually

Megan felt rather distant from God. She wanted to please him and worked very hard in her church. She was one of the 'doers' in the church. She was rather critical of some of her friends who she felt did so little. Any show of emotion bothered her and she did not like the emphasis on healing. She had been filled with the Spirit, but was worried in case things got out of control.

Listen for things heard in first interview

Thinking – 'I must be a success to win my father's approval'

'To be clever is to be valued'

'I must work hard to be loved and accepted'

Feelings

Anger (at failure). Fear (of being out of control). Anxiety (in case of failure). Sadness (at not being loved).

Behaviour

Megan is driven by her need to be loved and valued by her father. This causes her to try and be perfect and to make her children perfect. She is a workaholic and perfectionist as a result.

Possible way through for Megan?

In the counselling time work with Megan on her irrational beliefs – the tapes she is playing to herself. Look at God's unconditional love for her.

Give her homework that works on those beliefs. Practical homework may also help her. For example some relaxation with a friend could be beneficial.

In prayer time ask God to take Megan back to the painful memories of her childhood. Help her to express the pain to God – the pain of feeling such a failure; the pain of feeling unloved and unacceptable. Pray that God will come and show her his love and acceptance of her. Gradually, as feelings come out, lead her into forgiveness of her father.

Ask God to show her any 'inner vows' she may have made. She may need to renounce vows to be perfect and earn her father's love. When she does this, break the power of them.

Megan will need to look at her ungodly behaviour patterns. She may need to look at the idols in her life: success, her dad's approval. Pray through some of these issues with her and pray for repentance.

Be prepared to work with Megan for some months on all these issues and others that may come up.

Values in the Healing Ministry and Pastoral Prayer Ministry

The Authority of the Name of Jesus

We must start by knowing Jesus and, through him, the Father. In His name there is authority over the powers of darkness.

The Work of Christ on the Cross

On the cross, Jesus bore our infirmities, our sorrows and our transgressions. It was there that the ultimate victory over Satan was won – therefore the cross must be central in any ministry.

The Work of the Spirit

It is only God who ministers – his timing is perfect – we can't heal anyone.
The Holy Spirit is the active agent/representative of the Godhead at work in the world today. He dispenses power to use the gifts the risen Christ has bestowed upon us. It is his work, not ours. We must be Holy Spirit filled and focused.

The Word of God

All our ministry and practices must be in tune with the Word of God, never in contradiction to the clear teaching of scripture.

The Body of Christ

We need an ever deepening relationship in the body of Christ. Ministry should integrate a person, bringing wholeness to the individual and the local church.

The Growth of the Individual

Growth and maturity for the individual is the goal of ministry. With God's help we are seeking to remove whatever may block this.

Love

Every person is precious to God. We must therefore minister lovingly and sensitively, always seeking to respect the dignity of the individual.

Ref. 'Come Holy Spirit' Ch. 10; 'Set My People Free' Ch. 3.

SIX MONTHLY PLANNED PRAYER MINISTRY REVIEW SHEET

Date of Review _____

Please complete separate sheet if B is leading some sessions with someone else

A. Lead _____ B. Supported by _____

Address _____

_____ Phone _____

Please note if you are supported by someone different from B for any specific prayer

REVIEW OF CURRENT LOAD LISTED IN ORDER OF FREQUENCY OF SESSION

INDIVIDUAL (Note if married couple)	CHURCH OR FROM OUTSIDE	FREQUENCY	SUPPORT BY
REVIEW OF OTHERS YOU HAVE SEEN IN THE LAST 12 MONTHS ON A REGULAR BASIS (as opposed to one-off session)			

FUTURE POSITION I/we could see _____ more if required in the next three months.

On average we can see about _____ people each week

Books for further reading

All Alone, Help and Hope for Single Parents – Jill Worth & Christine Tufnell, Spring Harvest 2001, ISBN 0801056993

Helping victims of sexual abuse – Lynn Heitritter & Jeanette Vought, Bethany House Publishers, ISBN 0871239302

Touching: Human Significance of the Skin – Ashley Montagu, Harper Row 1986, ISBN 0060960280

Roots and Shoots updated edition – Roger Hurding, Hodder and Stoughton 2003, ISN 0340861495

Healing Life's Hurts – Dennis & Matthew Linn, ISBN 0809120593

Healing – Francis McNutt, Ava Maria Press, ISBN 340661402

The Road Less Travelled – M Scott-Peck, Hutchinson, ISBN 0712661158

Healing for Damaged Emotions – David Seaman, Victor Books, ISBN 0946515069

Putting Away Childish Things – David Seaman, Victor Books

The Secret Life of the Unborn Child – Thomas Verney, Delta ISBN 0440505658

Love is a choice – Dr Robert Hemfelt, Dr Fank, Dr Paul Meier, ISBN 185424602X

Restoring the Christian Soul Through Healing Prayer – Leanne payne, Kingsway ISBN 0801056993

Dying To Change – Mary Pytches, New Wine International Publishing, ISBN 190297705X

A Father's Place – Mary Pytches, New Wine International Publishing, ISBN 190297705X

Between Friends – Mary Pytches, New Wine International Publishing, ISBN 1902977041

Who Am I? – Mary Pytches, Kingdom Power Trust Publications, ISBN 0952641828

A Child No More – Mary Pytches, Kingdom Power Trust Publications, ISBN 09522641836

Yesterday's Child – Mary Pytches, Hodder & Stoughton, ISBN 0340522739

Come Holy Spirit – David Pytches, Kingdom Power Trust Publications, ISBN 095264181X

Will the Real Me Please Stand Up – John Powell, ISBN 0883437316X

Emotional Intelligence – Daniel Goleman, Bantam Books

Resources information

Note: This list has been compiled from personal recommendations but we have not always had direct experience of the organisations.

Acorn Christian Foundation (Training and support) Whitehill Chase, Bordon, Hampshire, GU35 0AP Tel: 01420 478121 www.acornchristian.org

Anorexia and Bulimia Care (Support and resources for sufferers and families) Providence House, The Borough, Wedmore, Somerset BS28 4EG Tel: 03000 11 12 13, www.anorexiabulimiacare.org.uk

Association of Christian Counsellors (ACC standards body for the accreditation of individuals and the recognition of training for organisations) 29 Momus Boulevard, Coventry CV2 5NA Tel: 0845 124 9569 / 9570 www.acc-uk.org

Beacon Foundation (National telephone helpline for survivors of ritual abuse and those supporting them) 3 Grosvenor Avenue, Rhyl LL18 4HA Tel: 01745 343600

Bereaved Parents' Network (support for parents who have experienced the death of a child) See 'Care for the family'

Bud Christian Trust, The (Care, support, training and counselling) 22 Hill House Street, Corbridge, Northumberland NE45 5AA Tel: 01434 633429

Cardiff Concern (Provides counselling based upon biblical principles to the community in the Cardiff area. Also offers an advanced training course) Regal House, Gelligaer Lane, Cathays, Cardiff, CF4 3JS. Tel: 029 2066 4410 www.cardiffconcern.org.uk

CARE (Christian Action Research and Education – lobbying, communicating and educating on social issues) 53 Romney Street, London SW1P 3RF Tel: 020 7233 0455 www.care.org.uk

Care for the Family (Support for families and through family break-ups) Garth House, Leon Avenue, Cardiff, CF15 7RG Tel: (029) 2081 0800 www.careforthefamily.org.uk

Catholic Marriage Centre (Courses for married couples who want to enrich, repair or rebuild their marriages) Oasis of Peace, Penamser Road,Porthmadog, Gwynedd, LL49 9NY Tel: 01766 514300 www.catholicmarriagecentre.org.uk

Christians in Caring Professions (CiCP) (Encouragement, traning and support) PO Box 2828, Reading, RG30 2GE Tel: 0118 959 5838 www.cicp.org.uk

Christian Fellowship of Healing, The (Prayer ministry and training) 6, Morningside Road, Edinburgh, EH10 4DD Tel: 0131 228 6553

Christian Healing Mission, The (Care, counselling and prayer) 8 Cambridge Court, 210 Shepherd's Bush Road, Hammersmith, London, W6 7NJ Tel: 020 7603 8118 www.healingmission.org

Churches Child Protection Advisory Service (CCPAS) (Training, support and advice for churches and organisations) PO Box 133, Swanley, Kent BR8 7UQ Tel: 0845 120 4550 Fax: 0845 120 4552 www.ccpas.co.uk

Bridge Pastoral Foundation 2 Gar Street, Winchester SO23 8GQ Tel: 01962 843040 www.bridgepastoral.org.uk

Cogwheel Trust (Care support and counselling, marriage and family issues) 47-51 Norfolk St, Cambridge CB1 2CD Tel: 01223 464385 Email: cwt@btconnect.com

Connect (Christian counselling service) 8 Portesbury Road, Camberley, Surrey, GU15 3TA Tel: 01276 24210 www.connectcounselling.org.uk

Credit Action (Support for people in debt and help with managing money) 6th Floor, Lynton House, 7-12 Tavistock Square, London WC1H 9LT Tel: 0207 380 3390. Email: office@creditaction.org.uk www.creditaction.org.uk

Crossline Coventry (Telephone listening and counselling service) Coventry City Mission, PO Box 40, Coventry, CV1 9DQ Tel: 024 7661 5931 Email: john@covcitymission.org.uk

Crossline Edinburgh (Telephone listening and counselling service) Edinburgh City Mission, 9 Pilrig Street, Edinburgh, EH6 5AH. Tel: 0131 554 6140 www.edinburghcitymission.org.uk

CWR (Crusade for World Revival) (Education and training in counselling, non-residential and residential courses) Waverley Abbey House, Waverley Lane, Farnham, Surrey, GU9 8EP Tel: 01252 784700 Email: info@cwr.org.uk www.cwr.org.uk

Ellel Ministries (Healing retreats, training and counselling) Ellel Grange, Bay House, Lancaster LA2 0HN Tel: 01524 751651 www.ellelministries.org.uk

Emmaus Counselling Service (Christian counselling service) St. Philip's House, Birken Road, Tunbridge Wells, Kent TN2 3TE Tel: 01892 861160

Harnhill Centre of Christian Healing (Residential training and counselling) Harnhill Manor, Cirencester, GL7 5PX Tel: 01285 850283 www.harnhillcentre.org.uk

House of Bread, The (Counselling and healing) Ross Road, Christchurch, Coleford, Glos. GL16 7NS Tel: 01594 837744 www.wflt.org

Kainos Trust for Eating Disorders (Services which help those with eating disorders to reach and maintain full recovery through teaching and counselling) The Lower George House, High Street, Newnham-on-Severn GL14 1BS Tel/Fax: 01594 516284

Kaleidoscope Project (Education, training & counselling in drug-related issues) 11A Charles St., Newport, South Wales NP20 1JU Tel: 0845 4506507 Email: kaleidoscope@blueyonder.co.uk

Kings Communications (Offers professional Christian counselling; training programmes for organisations and individuals) 1st Floor, Wakefield Building, Gomm Rd, High Wycombe HP13 7DJ Tel: 01494 512441 www.kingscommunications.com

Life for the World Trust (Help for victims of drug abuse and addictions) Wakefield Building, Gomm Rd, High Wycombe HP13 7DJ Tel: 01494 462008 www.lftw.org

Lighthouse Christian Care Ministry (Marriage counselling) 1a Argyll Street, Coventry CV2 4FJ Tel: 02476 440095 www.lighthousechristiancare.co.uk

Living Waters UK (Ministry, support and training on sexual and relational brokeness) PO Box 1530, London SW1 0WF Tel: 0207 799 2200 Email info@living-waters-uk.org

Manna House Counselling Service (Christian training and counselling service) The Manna House, 72 St. Giles Street, Northampton NN1 1JW Tel: 01604 633304 Email: mhcs@mannahouse.org.uk

Mildmay Mission Hospital (Christian hospital providing palliative care for those living with or affected by HIV & AIDS) Austin Street, London E2 7NB Tel: 020 7613 6300 www.mildmay.org

Mission to Marriage (Residential and church-based Christian marriage weekends, training and counselling) Tel: 01654 70265 Email: admin@christianmarriageministries.com www.christianmarriageministries.com

Mulberry House (Conference facilities) Mulberry House, Chelmsford Road, High Ongar, Essex CM5 9NL Tel: 01277 365398 www.mulberry-house.com

Nationwide Christian Helpline, The (Listening, help, support and prayer) Helpline: 08445 768876 www.nationwidechristiantrust.com

New Life Christian Centre
(Children's work and counselling service) 5 Cairo New Rd, Croydon, Surrey CR0 1XP Tel: 020 8680 7671 Email: enquiries@newlifecroydon.co.uk

Northumbrian Centre of Prayer for Christian Healing (Healing meetings, prayer ministry and teaching) Beggar's Roost, West Denton United Reformed Church, Middle Gate, West Denton, Newcastle upon Tyne NE5 5AY Tel: 01207 542374 www.christian-healing.com

Orpington Christian Counselling Service
(Christian counselling) 137 Crofton Lane, Petts Wood, Kent BR5 1HB Tel: 01689 852105

Oxford Christian Institute for Counselling (OCIC)
(counselling, coaching, retreats, workshops and training in pastoral care) The Priory Annexe, 85 Old High St, Headington, Oxford OX3 9HT Tel: 01865 308889 Email: counselling@ocic.org.uk www.ocic.org.uk

PCCA Christian Child Care
(See 'Churches Child Protection Advisory Service')

Pilgrims Hall (Residential training and retreat facilities) Ongar Road, Brentwood, Essex CM15 9SA Tel: 01277 372206 Email: team@pilgrimshall.org.uk www.pilgrimshall.co.uk

Reach Merseyside
(Hospitality, care and counselling) Reach Merseyside,

85a Allerton Road, Liverpool L18 2DA Tel: 0151 737 2121 Fax: 0151 737 2185 Email: reach@reachuk.co.uk www.reachuk.co.uk

St John's College (Pastoral counselling and healing: education and training) St John's College, Chilwell Lane, Bramcote, Nottingham NG9 3DS Tel: 0115 925 1114 www.stjohns-nottm.ac.uk

Scargill House (Education, training and recreation) Scargill House Ltd, Kettlewell, Skipton, North Yorkshire BD23 5HU Tel: 01756 761236 www.scargillmovement.org

Sevenoaks Christian Counselling Service
(Counselling Service) The Bridge, Littlecourt Road, Sevenoaks, kent TN13 2JG Tel: 01732 450118 www.sevenoakscounselling.org.uk

SOZO Ministries (Teaching and ministry) Sozo House, Alma Road, Romsey, Hampshire SO51 8ED Tel: 01794 522511 www.sozo.org

Swansea City Mission
(Christian resource and counseling centre) Nicholaston House, Penmaen, Gower, Swansea SA3 2HL Tel: 01792 371317

True Freedom Trust
(Teaching and counselling ministry on homosexuality and related issues) P.O. Box 13, Prenton, Wirral CH43 6BY Tel: 0151 653 0773 www.truefreedomtrust.co.uk

United Christian Healing Ministry (Christian counselling and training) 78 New Street, Milnsbridge, Huddersfield HD3 4LD Tel: 01484 461098 www.uchm.org

United Evangelical Project
(Counselling and training) 160 Hanstead Rd, Handsworth, Birmingham B20 2QR Tel: 0121 551 7984

The Waymark Trust
(counselling service. 24-hour answerphone) 1 Link Lane, Canterbury, Kent CT1 2AF Tel: 01227 781891

Well Counselling Service, The (Fellowship and counselling) The Lyttleton Rooms, Church Street, Malvern, Worcestershire WR14 2AY Tel: 01684 563456

Wellspring Christian Trust
(Counselling service) 61 Main Street, Frodsham, Cheshire WA6 7DF Tel: 01928 735589 www.wellspringchristiantrust.co.uk

Westminster Pastoral Foundation (Training, counselling and supervision) 23 Magdalen St, London SE1 2EN Tel: 0207 378 2000 www.wpf.org.uk

Whitchester Christian Centre (Counselling and training) Borthaugh, Hawick, Roxburghshire TD9 7LN Tel: 01450 377 477 www.whitchester.org.uk

New Wine Vision and Core Values

Our Vision

To see the nation changed through Christians experiencing the joy of worshipping God, the freedom of following Jesus, and the power of being filled with the Spirit.

To see churches renewed, strengthened and planted, living out the word of God in every aspect of life, serving God by reaching the lost, broken and poor, and demonstrating the good news of the Kingdom of God to all.

Our Values

Continuity & Change – we want to be faithful guardians of an unchanging message about the person and work of Jesus, and the need for personal salvation and sanctification, while also adapting ways of worship, teaching, being church and doing mission according to culture and context.

Cross & Resurrection – we want to honour all that Jesus has done for us on the cross, and to embrace the way of the cross for ourselves, while also knowing the power of his resurrection to set us free.

Gracious & Truthful – we want to be kind and generous in the way we think and speak about others whether they agree or disagree with us, while also clearly communicating what we believe and why we believe it.

Leadership & Every-member ministry – we want to train and deploy anointed, courageous and missional church leaders, while also equipping every Christian to serve like Jesus in their home, church, work and life-place.

Mission & Community – we want to see the church become a missionary movement to love and reach the lost, to care for the poor and to bring justice to our homes, neighbourhoods, workplaces and nations, while also being a grace-filled community in which people can find relationship, healing, faith, hope and love.

Natural & Supernatural – we want to see every Christian using all the natural reason, wisdom and skill that they can, while also learning to operate in the supernatural gifts of the Spirit to minister to others in love and power as Jesus did.

Now & Not yet of the Kingdom – we want to proclaim the good news of the Kingdom of God and to see that confirmed by miraculous signs and wonders, while also ministering grace to all, knowing that suffering will be part of life until Jesus returns and makes all things new.

Transcendence & Presence – we want to live lives that celebrate God's awesome power, transcendent majesty and sovereign work, while at the same time experiencing his intimate presence as we encounter him in heartfelt worship.

Unity & Diversity – we want to work with everyone who holds these values in open, mutually accountable friendship, while also acknowledging and honouring differences in leadership style, church characteristics and denominational emphasis.

Word & Spirit – we want to derive all we believe, teach and do from the Bible as the written word of God, while also learning to hear and obey the voice of the Spirit speaking to us individually and collectively.